USEFUL EXPRESSIONS

in SPANISH

FOR THE ENGLISH-SPEAKING TOURIST

Editors: A. Z. Stern — Joseph A. Reif, Ph.D.

Spanish

 ·K·U·P·E·R·A

© 1992 KS-JM Books

Distributed in the United Kingdom by:
Kuperard (London) Ltd.
No. 9 Hampstead West
224 Iverson Road
West Hampstead
London NW6 2HL

ISBN 1-870668-68-5

This booklet is an up-to-date and practical phrase book for your trip to Spain. It includes the phrases and vocabulary you will need in most of the situations in which you will find yourself, and it contains a pronunciation guide for all the material. Some of the phrases occur in more than one section so that you do not have to turn pages back and forth. At the beginning is a basic, general vocabulary with which you should become familiar, and at the end is a list of emergency expressions for quick reference.

The pronunciation of Spanish is fairly simple. Most of the sounds are very similar to English sounds, and you will quickly achieve an easily understandable accent. The transcription should be read as follows:

VOWELS: **a** as in father, but shorter

e as in let, sometimes more like **a** in late

i as in machine

o as in rope, sometimes like **aw** in saw

u as in tune

CONSONANTS: b, d, f, k, l, m, n, p, s, t, v, w, x, y, z, as in English

ch like as in church

g as in go, not as in gentle

th as in think, **not** as in then

dh like **th** in then

gh a weak, voiced version of the **ch** in Scottish loch

kh like **ch** in Scottish loch

r is trilled as in Scottish **r**

rr is strongly trilled

STRESS: In words ending with a consonant the last syllable is stressed. In words ending with a vowel the next to last syllable is stressed. Exceptions to this rule are marked with an acute accent in the transcription.

CONTENTS

Basic Dictionary	1	Airplane	40
First meeting: Greetings	10	Car journey	42
Hotel	12	Traffic signs	45
Information at hotel	16	Garage	47
Taxi	19	Repairs	48
In the post office	19	Parts of a car	50
In the restaurant	22	Physicians	51
Grocery	26	Types of doctors	51
Fruits and vegetables	27	Illnesses	52
Bank	29	Parts of the body	53
Clothes	30	Pharmacy	55
Colors	34	Time	56
Laundry	34	Days of the week	57
At the hairdresser	35	Months	58
Bookshop	36	Seasons	58
The Weather	37	Numbers	58
Transport	38	Emergency expressions	60
	38		

BASIC DICTIONARY	VOCABULARIO BÁSICO	BOKAVULARIO BASIKO
Thank you	Gracias	grathyas
Thank you very much	Muchas gracias	muchas grathyas
Please	Por favor	por favor
Excuse me	Discúlpeme	diskúlpeme
Never mind	No es nada	no es nadha
What? What is that?	¿Qué? ¿Qué es eso?	ke? ke es eso?
Where? Where is that?	¿Dónde? ¿Dónde está eso?	dónde? dónde esta eso?
When? How?	¿Cuándo? ¿Cómo?	kwando? kómo?
Which? Why?	¿Cuál? ¿Por qué?	kwal? por ke?
Is that?	¿Acaso es?	akaso es?
That is not	Eso no es	eso no es
Yes, no, perhaps	Sí, no, quizá	si, no, kithá
Correct, incorrect	Correcto, incorrecto	korekto, inkorekto
So so	Así así, regular	así así, reghular
Good, bad	Bien (bueno), mal (malo)	byen (bweno), mal (malo)
No good, not bad	No bueno, no malo	no bweno, no malo

There is, there is not (none)	Hay, no hay (nada)	ai, no ai (nadha)
I, you (m.s.) (f.s.)	Yo, tú	yo, tu
He, she	El, ella	el, elya
We, you	Nosotros, ustedes	nosotros, ustedhes
They (m.+f.)	Ellos, ellas	elyos, elyas
Mine, yours	Mío, tuyo (vuestro)	mío, tuyo (bwestro)
Ours, theirs	Nuestro, de ellos	nwestro, de elyos
At my place, at your place	En mi casa en tu casa	en mi kasa, en tu kasa
Wet, dry	Húmedo, seco	úmedho, seko
Old, new	Viejo, nuevo	byekho, nwevo
Pretty, not nice	Lindo, no lindo	lindo, no lindo
Much, few	Mucho, poco	mucho, poko
How many, How much	¿Cuánto?	kwánto?
Cheap, expensive	Barato, caro	barato, karo
Very expensive	Muy caro	muy karo
Free (of charge)	Gratis	gratis
More, less	Más, menos	mas, menos
Cheaper, more expensive	Más barato, más caro	mas barato, mas karo

Heavy, light	Pesado, liviano	pesadho, liviano
Now, at the same time as...	Ahora, al tiempo que...	aora, al tiempo ke ...
During	Durante	durante
Early, late	Más temprano (antes), más tarde (después)	mas temprano (antes), mas tarde (después)
On time, in time	A la hora debida (puntualmente)	a la ora devidha (puntualmente)
Here, there	Aquí, allá	aki, alyá
Inside, outside	Dentro de, fuera de (afuera)	dentro de, fuera de (afuera)
Up (stairs), down (stairs)	Hacia arriba, hacia abajo	athya arriva, athya avakho
To...	Hacia...	athya ...
Near, far	Cerca, lejos	therka, lekhos
In front of	Frente a	frente al
Behind (after)	Detrás (después)	detrás (después)
Sky	Cielo (firmamento)	thielo (firmamento)
Sun, moon	Sol, luna	sol, luna
Stars	Estrellas	estrelyas
Light, darkness	Luz, oscuridad	luth, oskuridhadh

Heat, cold, warm	Calor, frío, caliente	kalor, frío, kalyente
East, west	Este, oeste	este, oeste
North, south	Norte, sur	norte, sur
Rain, snow, wind	Lluvia, nieve, viento	lyuvia, nyeve, byento
Earth, mountain, valley	Tierra, montaña, valle	tyerra, montanya, valye
River, bridge	Río, puente	rio, pwente
Desert, sand	Desierto, arena	desyerto, arena
Sea, water, ship	Mar, agua, barco	mar, aghwa, barko
Country, place	País, lugar	país, lughar
City, village	Ciudad, aldea	thiudhadh, aldea
Road, street	Ruta (camino), calle	ruta (kamino), kalye
House, flat	Casa, departamento	kasa, departamento
Room, door	Habitación, puerta	avitathyón, pwerta
Key, lock	Llave, cerradura	lyave, therradhura
Wall, window	Pared (muro), ventana	paredh (muro), bentana
Roof, steps	Techo (tejado), escaleras (peldaños)	techo (tekhadho), escaleras (peldanyos)
Kitchen, toilet	Cocina, excusado	kothina, exkusadho

4

English	Spanish	Pronunciation
Bed, pillows	Cama, almohadones	kama, almo'adhones
Blanket, carpet	Manta (frazada), alfombra	manta (frathadha), alfombra
Wardobe	Ropero (armario)	ropero (armario)
Table, chair	Mesa, silla	mesa, silya
Man, woman	Hombre, mujer	ombre, mukher
Father, mother	Padre, madre	padre, madre
Son, daughter	Hijo, hija	ikho, ikha
Grandson, granddaughter	Nieto, nieta	nyeto, nyeta
Brother, sister	Hermano, hermana	ermano, ermana
Uncle, aunt	Tío, tía	tio, tia
Husband, wife	Esposo, esposa	esposo, esposa
Boy, girl	Niño, niña	ninyo, ninya
Old man, old woman	Anciano, anciana	anthiano, anthiana
To want	Querer	kerer
I want, You want	Quiero, quieres	kyero, kyeres
I wanted, you wanted	Quise, usted quiso	kise, ustedh kiso
I will want, you will want	Querré, querrás	kerré, kerrás
I do not want	No quiero	no kyero
To visit	Visitar	bisitar

I visit, you visit	Yo visito, usted visita	yo bisito, ustedh bisita
I visited, you visited	Visité, visitaste	bisité, bisitaste
I will visit, you will visit	Visitaré, visitarás	bisitaré, bisitarás
To speak	Hablar	ablar
I speak, you speak	Yo hablo, usted habla	yo ablo, ustedh abla
I spoke, you spoke	Hablé, usted habló	ablé, ustedh abló
I will speak, you will speak	Hablaré, usted hablará	ablaré, ustedh ablará
I do not speak	Yo no hablo	yo no ablo
To understand	Comprender	komprender
I understand, you understand	Comprendo, usted comprende	komprendo, ustedh komprende
I understood, you understood	Comprendí, usted comprendió	komprendí, ustedh komprendyó
I do not understand	No comprendo	no komprendo
To go	Ir	ir
I go, you go	Voy, usted va	boy, ustedh ba
I went, you went	Fui, usted ha ido	fwi, ustedh a idho
I will go, you will go	Iré, usted irá	iré, ustedh irá
I do not go	No voy	no boy
To travel	Viajar	byakhar

I travel, you travel	Viajo, usted viaja	byakho, ustedh byakha
I travelled, you travelled	Viajé, usted viajó	byakhé, usted byakhó
I will travel, you will travel	Viajaré, usted viajará	byakharé, ustedh byakhará
I do not travel	No viajo	no byakho
To stand	Estar de pie	estar de pye
I stand, you stand	Estoy de pie, estás de pie	estoy de pye, estás de pye
I stood, you stood	Estuve de pie, estuviste de pie	estuve de pye, estuviste de pye
I do not stand	No estoy de pie	no estoy de pye
To sleep	Dormir	dormir
I sleep, you sleep	Duermo, duermes	dwermo, dwermes
I slept, you slept	Dormí, usted durmió	dormi, ustedh durmyó
I will sleep, you will sleep	Dormiré, usted dormirá	dormiré, ustedh dormirá
I do not sleep	No duermo	no dwermo
To rest	Descansar	deskansar
I rest, you rest	Descanso, descansas	deskanso, deskansas
I rested, you rested	Descansé, descansaste	deskanse, deskansaste
I will rest, you will rest	Descansaré, descansarás	deskansaré, deskansarás
I do not rest	No descanso	no deskanso

English	Spanish	Pronunciation
To eat	Comer	komer
I eat, you eat	Como, comes	komo, komes
I ate, you ate	Comí, comiste	komí, komiste
I will eat, you will eat	Comeré, comerás	komeré, komerás
I do nót eat	No como	no komo
To drink	Beber	bever
I drink, you drink	Bebo, usted bebe	bevo, ustedh beve
I drank, you drank	Bebí, bebiste	beví, beviste
I will drink, you will drink	Beberé, beberás	beveré, beverás
I do not drink	No bebo	no bevo
To be afraid	Temer	temer
I am afraid, you are afraid	Temo, usted teme	temo, ustedh teme
I was afraid, you were afraid	Temí, usted temió	temí, ustedh temyó
I will be afraid	Temeré	temeré
You will be afraid	Usted temerá	ustedh temerá
I am not afraid	No temo	no temo
Don't be afraid	No tener miedo	no tener myedho
To hurry	Apurarse	apurarse
I am in a hurry	Tengo apuro	tengo apuro

8

English	Spanish	Pronunciation
You are in a hurry	Tienes apuro	tyenes apuro
I hurried, you hurried	Me apuré, te apuraste	me apuré, te apuraste
I will hurry, you will hurry	Me apuraré, te apurarás	me apuraré, te apurarás
I am not in a hurry	No tengo apuro	no tengo apuro
To ask for help	Pido ayuda	pidho ayudha
I ask for help	Necesito ayuda	nethesito ayudha
You ask for help	Necesitas ayuda	nethesitas ayudha
I asked for help	Pedí ayuda	pedhi ayudha
You asked for help	Usted pidió ayuda	ustedh pidhyó ayudha
I am not asking for help	No necesito pedir ayuda	no nethesito pedhir ayudha
Passport	Pasaporte	pasaporte
Flight	Vuelo	bwelo
Outgoing flight	Vuelo de partida	bwelo de partidha
Following flight	Vuelo de llegada	bwelo de lyeghadha
Flight number	Vuelo número	bwelo número
Suitcase	Maleta	maleta
Customs	Aduana	adhwana
Money	Dinero	dinero

FIRST MEETING, GREETINGS	PRIMERA ENTREVISTA, SALUDOS	PRIMERA ENTREVISTA, SALUDHOS
Hello!	¡Hola!	ola!
Good morning	Buen día	bwen día
Good evening	Buenas tardes	bwenas tardes
Good night	Buenas noches	bwenas noches
Welcome!	¡Bienvenido!	byenvenidho!
My name is ...	Me llamo...	me lyamo
I am from the United-States	Soy de los Estados Unidos	soy de los estadhos unidhos
I speak only English	Sólo hablo inglés	solo ablo inglés
I am pleased to meet you	Me alegro de verlo	me alegro de berlo
How are you?	¿Cómo le va?	komo le ba?
Fine, thank you, And how are you?	Bien, gracias, ¿y a usted?	byen, grathyas, i a ustedh?
How are things?	¿Cómo van las cosas?	komo ban las kosas?
All right	Todo en orden	todho en orden
I've come to learn about country	Vine para conocer su país	bine para konother su país

10

English	Spanish	Pronunciation
I've come on a vacation	Vine de vacaciones	bine de bakathyones
Is there someone here who speaks English?	¿Hay alguien aquí que hable inglés?	ai algien aki ke able ingles?
Yes, no	Sí, no	si, no
I don't speak Spanish	Yo no hablo español	yo no ablo espanyol
I speak English	Yo hablo inglés	yo ablo inglés
I speak a little	Hablo un poco	ablo un poko
Do you understand me?	¿Usted me comprende?	ustedh me komprende?
I understand a little	Comprendo un poco	komprendo un poko
Pardon, excuse me	Perdón, dispénseme	perdon, dispénseme
I am sorry	Lo siento	lo syento
It doesn't matter	No es nada	no es nadha
Thank you very much	Muchas gracias	muchas grathyas
Don't mention it	No hable más de eso	no able mas de eso
What do you want?	¿Qué quiere usted?	ke kyere ustedh?
I would like to visit the city	Quisiera visitar la ciudad	kisyera bisitar la thiudhadh
Wait a minute!	¡Espere un momento!	espere un momento!
Come with me!	¡Venga conmigo!	benga konmigho

I have to leave now	Yo me tengo que ir	yo me tengo ke ir
Thank you for your attention	Gracias por su gentileza	grathyas por su khentiletha
Good luck!	¡Buena suerte!	bwena swerte!
See you later!	¡Hasta la vista!	asta la bista!
Goodbye!	Adiós	adhyos

HOTEL

HOTEL	HOTEL

I am looking for a good hotel	Estoy buscando un buen hotel	estoy buskando un bwen hotel
I am looking for an inexpensive hotel	Estoy buscando un hotel no costoso	estoy buskando un otel no kostoso
I booked a room here, is it ready?	Encargué aquí una habitación, ¿está lista?	enkargé aki una abitathyón, esta lista?
Have you a single room? A double room?	¿Tiene una habitación para una sola persona? ¿Para una pareja?	tyene una abitathyón para una sola persona? para una parekha?
Have you a better room?	¿Tiene una habitación mejor?	tyene una abitathyón mekhor?
Is the room air-conditioned?	¿La habitación es con aire acondicionado?	la abitathyón es con aire akondithyonadho?

Does the room have a shower?	¿Hay bañadera en la habitación?	ai banyadhera en la abitathyón?
With breakfast?	¿Con desayuno?	kon desayuno?
How much is the room?	¿Cuál es el precio de la habitación?	kwal es el prethyo de la abitathyón?
I should like to see the room	Me gustaría ver la habitación	me gustaría ber la abitathyón
Do you have something bigger? Smaller? Cheaper? Quieter?	¿Tiene algo más grande? ¿Más pequeño? ¿Más barato? ¿Más tranquilo?	tyene algo mas grande? mas pekenyo? mas barato? mas trankilo?
Will you send for my bags?	¿Puede mandar a traer mis valijas?	pwedhe mandar a traer mis balikhas?
I would like to keep this in the safe	Quisiera guardarlo en el depósito	kisyera gwardarlo en el déposito
Where is the ladies room? The men's room?	¿Dónde está el cuarto de mujeres? ¿El cuarto de hombres?	donde está el kwarto de mukheres? el kwarto de ombres?
Where is the dining room? T.V. Room?	¿Dónde está la sala-comedor? ¿La sala de TV?	donde está la sala komedhor? la sala de televisyón?

Please, wake me at ...	Por favor, despiérteme a...	por favor, despyérteme a ...
Who's there? Please wait!	¿Quién es? ¡Espere por favor!	kyen es? espere por favor!
Come in!	¡Entre!	entre!
May I have another towel?	¿Puedo recibir otra toalla?	pwedho rethivir otra toalya?
May I have another pillow?	¿Puedo recibir otro almohadón?	pwedo réthivir otro almo'adhon?
... another blanket?	... otra manta?	... otra manta?
... hangers?	... perchas?	... perchas?
... hot water bottle?	... una botella de agua caliente?	... una botelya de aghwa kalyente?
... night lamp?	... un velador de noche?	... un beladhor de noche?
... needle and thread?	... una aguja y tela de algodón?	... una aghukha i tela de algodhón?
... writing paper?	... papel para escribir?	... papel para eskrivir?
... pen?	... lapicero?	... lapithero?
Could you cable abroad for me?	¿Podría mandarme un telegrama al exterior?	podria mandarme un teleghrama al exterior?
A vacant room	Una habitación desocupada	una abitathyón desokupadha

Receptionist	El recepcionista	el rethepthyonista;
Chambermaid	La camarera	la kamarera
Security officer	El oficial de seguridad	el ofithyal de seghuridhadh;
Waiter	El camarero (mozo)	el kamarero (motho)
Dining room	La Sala Comedor	la sala-komedhor
Reception room	La Sala de Recepción	la sala de rethepthyón
Lift boy (elevator boy)	El ascensorista	el asensorista
Room key	Llavė de la habitación	lyave de la abitathyón
Room number	Número de la habitación	numero de la abitathyón
Bed	Cama	kama
Blanket	Manta (frazada)	manta (frathadha)
Sheet	Sábana	sávana
Mens toilet, ladies' toilet	Baño de hombres, baño de mujeres	banyo de ombres, banyo de mukheres
Toilet paper	Papel tualete	papel twalete

INFORMATION AT HOTEL	INFORMACIÓN RECIBIDA EN EL HOTEL	INFORMATHYON RETHIVIDHA EN EL OTEL
Is there a taxi station nearby?	¿Hay una estación de taxis aquí cerca?	ai una estathyón de taxis akí therka?
What is the telephone number?	¿Qué número de teléfono tiene?	ke número de teléfono tyene?
How do I get to ...?	¿Cómo llego a...?	komo lyegho a...?
By bus? Where is the bus stop?	¿En autobús? ¿Dónde para el autobús?	en autovús? donde para el autovús?
Where is the nearest post office?	¿Dónde está la oficina de correo más cercana?	donde está la ofithina de korreo mas therkana?
Ladies hairdresser	Peluquero de mujeres	pelukero de mukheres
Barber	Barbero	barbero
Laundry, shop	Lavandería; tienda	lavandería; tyenda
Where can I get a snack?	¿Dónde puedo pedir una comida ligera?	donde pwedho pedhir una komidha lighera?
Is there a grocery nearby?	¿Hay un almacén por aquí cerca?	ai un almathén por akí therka?

16

English	Spanish	Pronunciation
Where is the Tourist Information Office?	¿Dónde está la Oficina de Información Turística?	donde está la ofithina de informathyón turistika?
Can I have a programme of this week's events?	¿Puedo recibir el programa de espectáculos de la semana?	pwedho rethivir el proghrama de espektákulos de la semana?
How can I get to...?	¿Cómo puedo llegar de aquí	komo pwedho lyeghar de aki a
...on foot?	...a pie?	...a pye?
...by bus?	...en autobús?	...en autovús?
...to this address?	...a esta dirección?	...a esta direkthyón?
...to the center of town?	...al centro de la ciudad?	...al thentro de la thiundhadh?
...to the shopping district?	...al centro de los negocios?	...al thentro de los neghothyos?
...to the bookshop?	...a una librería?	...a una libreria?
...to the market?	...al mercado?	...al merkadho?
...exhibitions?	...exposición?	...exposithyones?
...museum?	...al museo?	...al museo?
...to the theatre? cinema?	...al teatro? al cine?	...al teatro? al thine?
...to a nightclub?	...al club nocturno?	...al klub nokturno?

17

What plays are running this week?	¿Qué funciones son ofrecidas esta semana?	ke funthyones son ofrethidhas esta semana?
Which films worth seeing are on this week?	¿Qué películas que valga la pena ver se proyectan esta semana?	ke películas ke balgha la pena ber se proyektan esta semana?
Is there a tennis court nearby?	¿Hay una cancha de tenis aquí cerca?	ai una kancha de tenis aki therka?
Have you got any mail for me?	¿Recibió algún correo para mí?	rethivyó algún korreo para mi?
Is there a message for me?	¿Hay algún mensaje para mí?	ai algún mensakhe para mi?
I am going out and will return at …	Salgo y volveré a…	salgo i bolberé a …
I'll leave the hotel tomorrow at …	Dejaré el hotel mañana a las…	dekharé el otel manyana a las …
Please make up my bill	Sírvase hacerme la cuenta	sírbase atherme la kwenta
May I store my luggage here until …?	¿Puedo dejar mis cosas aquí hasta…?	pwedho dekhar mis kosas akí asta …?
Goodbye	¡Adiós, hasta la vista!	adhyós, asta la bista!

TAXI

Please call me a taxi

Driver, would you please bring my suitcase inside?

Take me to this address, please ...

Please, drive more slowly

How much is the fare?

Can you come here at ... in order to take me back?

TAXI

Por favor, encárgueme un taxi

Chofer, sírvase ayudarme a entrar la valija

Lléveme a esta dirección, por favor...

Por favor, maneje más lentamente

¿Cuánto debo pagar?

¿Puede volver aquí a las...para llevarme de regreso?

TAXI

por favor, enkárgweme un taxi

chofer, sírbase ayudharme a entrar la balikha

lyéveme a esta direkthyón, por favor ...

favor, manekhe mas lentamente

kwanto devo paghar?

pwedhe bolber akí a las ...para lyevarme de regreso?

IN THE POST OFFICE

Where is the post office?

Where can I send an overseas cable?

EN LA OFICINA DE CORREO

¿Dónde está la Oficina de Correo?

¿Dónde puedo mandar un telegrama al exterior?

EN LA OFITHINA DE KORREO

donde está la ofithina de korreo?

donde pwedho mandar un teleghrama al exterior?

English	Spanish	Pronunciation
Please, give me an overseas cable form	Por favor, deme un formulario para un telegrama al exterior	por favor, deme un formulario para un teleghrama al exterior
Have I Written the telegram clearly?	¿He escrito claramente el telegrama?	e eskrito klaramente el teleghrama?
When will the telegram arrive?	¿Cuándo llegará el telegrama?	kwando lyeghará el teleghrama?
How much do I have to pay?	¿Cuánto debo pagar?	kwanto devo paghar?
What stamps do I need for this letter by ordinary mail?	¿Qué estampillas necesito para mandar esta carta por correo común?	ke estampilyas nethesito para mandar esta karta por korreo komún?
...by air mail?	...por correo aéreo?	...por korreo aéreo?
...by registered mail?	...por certificado?	...por thertifikadho?
...by express delivery?	...por via expreso?	..por bia expreso?
Please send this registered	Por favor, mande esto por certificado	por favor, mande esto por thertifikadho
Please give me... postcards to send locally.	Sírvase darme...tarjetas postales para mandar en el país	sírbase darme ...tarkhetas postales para mandar en el país

Give me airletters to Europe, America, please	Por favor, deme aerogramas para Europa, América	por favor, deme aeroghramas para europa, amerika
Where is the nearest post box?	¿Dónde está el buzón más cercano?	donde está el buthón mas therkano
May I have some telephone tokens, please?	¿Puedo conseguir algunos cospeles para el teléfono?	pwedho konsegwir algunos kospeles para el teléfono?
Please, could you get me this number, as I could not get it by dialing?	Por favor, puede darme este número, yo no logro comunicarme?	por favor, pwed darme este número, yo no logro komunikarme?
Please, could you put me through to the International Exchange for this number?	Por favor, ¿podría comunicarme con la Central Internacional para este número?	por favor, podría komunikarme kon la thentral internathyonal para este número?
Please book me a call for tomorrow at ...	¿Quisiera encargarme una llamada para mañana, a...?	kisyera enkargharme una lyamadha para manyana a..?
I've come for my overseas call, booked for ... (hr.)	Vengo por mi llamada al exterior, encargada para (hora)	bengo por mi lyamadha al exterior, enkarghadha para (ora)

21

I'll be waiting here. Please call me when you get the connection	Esperaré aquí. Sírvase avisarme cuando consiga la comunicación	esperaré aki. sirbase avisarme kwando konsigha la komunikathyón
How much do I have to pay?	¿Cuánto debo pagar?	kwanto devo paghar?
Please, may I have a receipt?	Por favor, ¿puede darme un recibo?	por favor, pwedhe darme un rethivo
Thank you, goodbye	Gracias, Adiós	grathyas, adhyos

IN THE RESTAURANT

EN EL RESTAURANTE

EN EL RESTAURANTE

I am hungry	Tengo hambre	tengo ambre
I am thirsty	Tengo sed	tengo sedh
Where is there a good restaurant?	¿Dónde hay un buen restaurante?	donde ai un bwen restaurante?
Waiter	Mozo	motho
Waitress	Moza	motha
Can I see the menu?	¿Puedo ver el menú?	pwedho ber el menu?
Breakfast	Desayuno	desayuno

22

English	Español	Pronunciation
Lunch	Almuerzo	almwertho
Dinner	Cena	thena
I would like to order	Quisiera encargar	kisyera enkarghar
Give me this	Deme esto	deme esto
Tea with lemon, tea with milk	Té con limón, té con leche	te kon limón, te kon leche
Coffe and milk, Turkish coffee	Café con leche, café a la turca	kafé kon leche, kafé a la turka
Nescafe and milk	Nescafé con leche	neskafe kon leche
Milk, cocoa, espresso	Leche, cacao, expreso	leche, kakao, expreso
Cold, warm, hot	Frío, caliente, caluroso	frío, kaliente, kaluroso
Cold water, soda water	Agua fría, agua de soda	aghwa fría, aghwa de sodha
Orange juice, grapefruit juice	Jugo de naranja, jugo de toronja	khugho de narankha, khugho de toronkha
Cake, ice-cream	Bizcocho, helado	bithkocho, eladho
White beer, black beer	Cerveza blanca, cerveza negra	therbetha blanka, therbetha negra
Sweet wine, dry wine	Vino dulce, vino seco	bino dulthe, bino seko
Cognac, Whisky, arak	Coñac, wisky, arak	konyak, wiski, arak
Buttered roll	Panecillo con manteca	panethilyo kon manteka

23

Roll and margarine	Panecillo con margarina	panethilyo kon margharina
White bread, black bread	Pan blanco, pan negro	pan blanko, pan negro
Pita, toast and jam	Pita, tostada con compota	pita, tostadha kon kompota
Rolls	Panecillos	panethilyos
Egg, soft-boiled egg	Huevo, huevo pasado por agua	wevo, wevo pasadho por aghwa
Omelette, fried egg	Tortilla de huevos, huevo frito	tortilya de wevos, wevo frito
White cheese, yellow cheese	Queso blanco, queso amarillo	keso blanko, keso amarilyo
Leben, yogurt, sour-cream	Cuajada, yogurt, crema agria	kwakhadha, yogurt, krema aghria
Sausage, hot dogs	Salchicha, salchicha caliente	salchicha, salchicha kalyente
Vegetable salad	Ensalada de verduras	ensaladha de berduras
Salt, oil, sugar	Sal, aceite, azúcar	sal, atheite, athúkar
Pepper, lemon juice	Pimienta, jugo de limón	pimyenta, khugho de limón
Olives, pickled cucumber	Aceitunas, pepinillos encurtidos	atheitunas, pepinilyos enkurtidhos
Herring, pickled fish	Arenque, pescado en escabeche	arenkwe, peskadho en eskabeche

24

Smoked fish	Pescado ahumado	paskadho a'umadho
Bakala, filleted fish	Bacalao, filete de pescado	bakalao, filete de peskadho
Baked, filled carp	Cocido al horno, filete de carpa	kothidho al orno, filete de karpa
Baked, grilled, boiled	Cocido al horno, asado en parrilla, hervido	kothidho al orno, asadho en parrilya, erbidho
Fried, steamed	Frito, preparado con vapor	frito, preparadho kon bapor
Chicken, turkey, duck	Pollo, pavo, pato	polyo, pavo, pato
Beef, lamb	Carne de vaca, cordero	karne de baca, kordero
Liver, tongue	Higado, lengua	ighadho, lengwa
Steak, shnitzel	Biftec, milanesa	biftek, milanesa
Meat balls	Albóndigas	albóndighas
Beans soup, vegetable soup	Sopa de habas, sopa de verdura	sopa de avas, sopa de berdura
Chicken soup, meat soup	Sopa de pollo, sopa de carne	sopa de polyo, sopa de karne
Mashed potatoes	Papas mondadas	papas mondadhas
Chips	Papas fritas	papas fritas

Fruit salad	Ensalada de frutas	ensaladha de frutas
Pudding, bavaria cream	Budín, crema de Baviera	budhin, krema de bavyera
Glass, bottle, cup	Vidrio, botella, copa	bidrio, botelya, kopa
Spoon, fork, knife	Cuchara, tenedor, cuchillo	kuchara, tenedhor, kuchilyo
Plate, teaspoon	Plato, cucharita	plato, kucharita
Serviette, ashtray	Servilleta, cenicero	serbilyeta, thenithero
Toothpicks	Escarbadientes	eskarbadhyentes
How much must I pay?	¿Cuánto debo pagar?	kwanto devo paghar?
Change and a receipt, please	El vuelto y un recibo, por favor	el bwelto i un rethivo, por favor

GROCERY

DESPENSA

DESPENSA

White bread, brown bread	Pan blanco, pan oscuro	pan blanko, pan oskuro
Milk, leben, yogurt	Leche, cuajada, yogurt	leche, kwakhadha, yogurt
Sour cream, white cheese	Crema agria, queso blanco	krema aghria, keso blanko
Yellow cheese, salt cheese	Queso amarillo, queso salado	keso amarilyo, keso saladho
Butter, margarine, oil	Manteca, margarina, aceite	manteka, margharina, atheite

English	Español	(Phonetic)
Sardines, tuna fish, tuna salad	Sardinas, pescado tuna, ensalada de tuna	sardinas, peskadho tuna, ensaladha de tuna
Olives, eggs	Aceitunas, huevos	atheitunas, wevos
Soup mix	Sopa mixta	sopa mixta
Sugar, honey, salt	Azúcar, miel, sal	athúkar, myel, sal
Preserved meat	Carne en conserva	karne en konserba
Laundry soap	Jabón de lavar	khabón de lavar
Flour, noodles	Harina, fideos	arina, fidheos
Please give me	Sírvase darme...	sírbase darme ...
How much does it cost?	¿Cuánto...cuesta?	kwanto ...kwesta?

FRUITS AND VEGETABLES / FRUTAS Y VEGETALES / FRUTAS I BEKHETALES

English	Español	(Phonetic)
Almonds	Almendras	almendras
Apples	Manzanas	manthanas
Apricot	Damascos	damaskos
Banana	Banana	banana
Beans	Habas	avas

Beetroot	Remolacha	remolacha
Cabbage	Repollo	repolyo
Carrot	Zanahoria	thana'orya
Cauliflower	Coliflor	koliflor
Corn	Maíz	maith
Cucumber	Pepino	pepino
Dates	Dátil	dátil
Eggplant	Berenjena	berenkhena
Figs	Higos	ighos
Garlic	Ajo	akho
Grapefruit	Toronja	toronkha
Grapes	Uvas	uvas
Lemon	Limón	limón
Lettuce	Lechuga	lechugha
Squash	Calabaza	kalabatha
Melon	Melón	melón
Nuts	Nueces	nwethes
Onion	Cebolla	thevolya

Oranges	Naranjas	narankhas
Peaches	Duraznos	durathnos
Pears	Peras	peras
Peas	Guisantes	gwisantes
Pepper	Pimienta	pimyenta
Pomegranate	Granada	granadha
Potatoes	Papas	papas
Radish	Rábano	rávano
Rice	Arroz	arroth
Spinach	Espinaca	espinaka
Tomatoes	Tomates	tomates
Watermelon	Sandía	sandía

BANK	**BANCO**	**BANKO**
Where is the nearest bank?	¿Dónde está el banco más cercano?	donde está el banko mas therkano?
I have dollars to exchange	Tengo dólares para cambiar	tengo dólares para kambyar

Travellers checks	Cheques de viajeros	chekes de byakheros
Will you please change... dollars into local currency for me?	¿Por favor, quiere cambiarme dólares por moneda local?	por favor, kyere kambyarme dólares por monedha lokal?
Could I have it in small change, please?	¿Puede darme por favor cambio chico?	pwedhe darme por favor kambyo chiko?
... in large notes?	en billetes grandes?	en bilyetes grandes?
Could you, please, give me change for this note?	¿Por favor, puede cambiarme este billete?	por favor, pwedhe kambyarme este bilyete?
Cash, checks	Dinero en efectivo, cheque	dinero en efektivo, cheke
Clerk, manager	Empleado, Director	empleadho, direktor
Cash desk, cashier	Caja, cajero	kakha, kakhero

CLOTHES

ROPAS

ROPAS

I would like to buy...	Me gustaría comprar...	me gustaria komprar...
My size is ... My number is ...	Mis medidas son... Mi número es...	mis medhidhas son ...mi número es ...
May I try it on?	¿Puedo probarlo?	pwedho provarlo?

This is too short, too long	Esto es demasiado corto, demasiado largo	esto es demasyadho korto, demasyadho largo
It is too narrow, too wide	Esto demasiado angosto, demasiado ancho	es demasyadho angosto, demasyadho ancho
I would like to have it shortened	Me gustaría que fuera más corto	me gustaría ke fwera mas korto
A pair of shorts	Un par de calzones cortos	un par de kalthones kortos
A pair of trousers	Un par de pantalones	un par de pantalones
Boots	Botas	botas
Brassiere	Corpiño	korpinyo
Button	Botón	boton
Cape	Capa	kapa
Coat	Chaqueta	chaketa
Collar	Cuello	kwelyo
Cotton material	Material de algodón	material de alghodhón
Dress	Vestido (traje)	bestidho (trakhe)
Gloves	Guantes	gwantes
Hat	Sombrero	sombrero

Handkerchief	Pañuelo	panywelo
Jacket	Chaqueta	chaketa
Ladies handbag	Maleta de mujeres	maleta de mukheres
Leather	Cuero	kwero
Linen	Lino	lino
Nylon stockings	Medias de nylon	medhias de nailon
Night shirt	Camisa de dormir	kamisa de dormir
Pocket	Bolsillo	bolsilyo
Pantyhose	Media enteriza	medhia enteritha
Pajamas	Pijama	pikhama
Raincoat	Impermeable	impermeable
Robe	Bata	bata
Rubber boots	Zapatillas de goma	thapatilyas de goma
Sandals	Sandalias	sandalyas
Scarf	Bufanda	bufanda
Scissors	Tijeras	tikheras
Shoe laces	Cordones de zapatos	kordones de thapatos
Shoes	Zapatos	thapatos

Silk	Seda	sedha
Skirt	Camisa	kamisa
Skullcap	Casquete	kaskete
Slippers	Chinelas	chinelas
Sports shoes, sneakers	Zapatos de deporte, zapatos de gimnasia	thapatos de deporte, thapatos de khimnasya
Stockings	Medias	medhias
Sweater	Suéter	sweter
Swimsuit	Traje de baño	trakhe de banyo
Suit	Traje completo (conjunto)	trakhe kompleto (konkhunto)
Synthetic material	Material sintético	material sintétiko
Belt	Hilo	ilo
Tie	Nudo	nudho
Umbrella	Paraguas	paraghwas
Underpants	Calzoncillos	kalthonthilyos
Velvet	Terciopelo	terthiopelo
Undershirt	Camiseta (chaleco)	kamiseta (chaleko)
Woolen material	Material de lana	material de lana
Zipper	Cierre (cierre relámpago)	thyerre (thyerre relámpagho)

COLORS

I want a light shade,
   dark shade
Red, yellow
Green, blue
Purple, gray
Black, white
Brown, pink

COLORES

Quiero un matiz claro,
   matiz oscuro
Rojo, amarillo
Verde, azul
Púrpura, gris
Negro, blanco
Marrón, rosa

KOLORES

kyero un matith klaro,
   matith oskuro
rokho, amarilyo
berde, athul
púrpura, gris
negro, blanko
marrón, rosa

LAUNDRY

Could you please clean my
   suit?
Coat? Sweater?
Please, could you wash and
   iron the shirts and
   underwear for me?
When will they be ready for
   me?

LAVANDERÍA

¿Puede lavarme el traje, por
   favor?
¿Chaqueta? ¿Suéter?
¿Por favor, pueden lavarme y
   plancharme las camisas y la
   ropa interior?
¿Cuándo pueden estar listas?

LAVANDERÍA

pwedhe lavame el trakhe, por
   favor?
chaketa? swéter?
por favor, pwedhen lavarme i
   plancharme, las kamisas i la
   ropa interior?
kwando pwedhen estar listas?

Please, also do any necessary repairs	Sírvase hacer también los arreglos necesarios	sírbase ather también los arreglos nethesarios
The belt of the dress is missing	El cinturón del vestido se ha perdido	el thinturó del bestidho se a perdidho

AT THE HAIRDRESSER

EN LA PELUQUERÍA

EN LA PELUKERÍA

I want to get a hair cut	Quiero cortarme el cabello	keyro kortarme kavelyo
In front, on the sides, behind	Adelante, a los costados, atrás	adhelante, a los kistadhos atrás
Shorter, longer	Más corto, más largo	mas korto, mas largo
Side locks, beard, moustache	Patillas, barba, bigote	patilyas, harba, bighote
How long must I wait?	¿Cuánto tengo que esperar?	kwanto tengo ke esperar?
A short while, a long time	Un ratito, un tiempo largo	un ratito, un tyempo largo
I want a shampoo, please	Quiero un lavado de cabeza, por favor	kyero un lavadho de kavetha, por favor
The water is too hot	El agua está muy caliente	el aghwa está muy kalyente
I want a shave	Quiero afeitarme	kyero afeitarme
Be careful here!	¡Tenga cuidado aquí!	tenga kwidhadho aki!

35

English	Español	Pronunciation
I want my hair dyed	Quiero teñirme el cabello	kyero tenyirme el kavelyo
I want my hair set	Quiero arreglarme el cabello	kyero arreghlarme el kavelyo
Pedicure, manicure	Pedicuro, manicura	pedhikuro, manikura

BOOKSHOP / LIBRERÍA / LIBRERÍA

I would like to buy...	Quisiera comprar...	kisyera komprar...
...a newspaper	...un diario	...un diario
...a magazine	...una revista	...una revista
...a guidebook	...una guía	...una gia
...a map of the city	...un mapa de la ciudad	...un mapa de la thiudhadh
...a map of the country	...un mapa del país	...un mapa del pais
...envelopes	...sobres	...sobres
...a writing pad	...bloc de papel	...blok de papel
...an exercise book	...un cuaderno	...un kwaderno
...a pencil	...un lapicero	...un lapithero
...a fountain pen	...una lapicera fuente	...un lapithera fwente
...a ballpoint pen	...un lapicero a bolilla	...un lapithero a bolilya

THE WEATHER	TEMPERATURA	TEMPERATURA
What a beautiful day!	¡Qué día hermoso!	ke día ermoso!
Bright, the sun is shining	Claro, el sol brilla	klaro, el sol brilya
Warm, hot,	Cálido, caluroso,	kálidho, kaluroso,
very hot	muy caluroso	muy kaluroso
Chilly, cold, very cold	Fresco, frío, muy frio	fresko, frio, muy frio
Dry, heat wave	Seco, ola de calor	seko, ola de kalor
Damp, drizzle	Húmedo, llovizna	úmedho, lyovithna
It is raining	Lluvia	lyuvia
Cloudy, foggy	Nublado, hay neblina	nubladho, ai neblina
To wear a warm coat	Vestir una chaqueta abrigada	bestir una chaketa abrighadha
Raincoat, cape	Impermeable, capa	impermeable, kapa
Rubber boots	Botas de goma	botas de goma
To take an umbrella, parasol	Llevar un paraguas, una sombrilla	lyevar un paraghwas, una sombrilya

TRANSPORT	**TRANSPORTE**	**TRANSPORTE**
Bus, train, plane	Autobús, tren, avión	autovús, tren, avyón
Underground, express train	Subterráneo, tren expreso	suvteraneo, tren expreso
Ticket, ticket office	Boleto (pasaje), oficina de pasajes	boleto (pasakhe), ofithina de pasakhes
Driver, steward, stewardess	Conductor, camarero, azafata	konduktor, kamarero, athafata
Load/luggage, porter	Carga/equipaje, portero	karga/ekipakhe, portero
Where is the lost baggage office?	¿Dónde está la oficina de equipajes perdidos?	donde está la ofithina de ekipakhes perdidhos?
I left ... in the coach	Lo olvidé...en el coche	lo olbidhe ...en el koche

TRAIN · TREN · TREN

TRAIN	**TREN**	**TREN**
When does the train for ... leave?	¿Cuándo el tren para...? ¿parte a?	kwando el tren para ...? parte a?
How do I get there?	¿Cómo llego ahí?	komo lyegho a'i?
By train, bus, underground (Subway)	¿En tren, en autobús, en subterráneo?	en tren, en autovús, en suvteraneo?

Where is the ticket office?	¿Dónde está la oficina de pasajes?	donde está la ofithina de pasakhes?
At what time does the next train leave for ...?	¿A qué hora parte el próximo tren a...?	a ke ora parte el próximo tren a ...?
Give me a ticket for ... please	Deme un pasaje a...por favor	deme un pasakhe a ...por favor
If possible, by the window and facing the front	Si es posible junto a la ventana y mirando al frente	si es posible khunto a la bentana i mirando al frente
Where can I find a porter?	¿Dónde puedo hallar un changador?	donde pwedho alyar un changadhor?
Please, take the bags to the coach	Por favor, lleve las valijas al coche	por favor, lyeve las balikhas al koche
Where is the dining coach?	¿Dónde está el vagón comedor?	donde está el baghón komedhor?
May I open (close) the window?	¿Puedo abrir (cerrar) la ventana?	pwedho abrir (therrar) la bentana?
May I smoke?	¿Puedo fumar?	pwedho fumar?
When does the train arrive at?	¿Cuándo llega el tren a...?	kwando lyegha el tren a ...?
What bus goes to...?	¿Qué autobús lleva a...?	ke autovús lyeva a ...?

39

Where is the bus to ...?	¿Dónde se toma el autobús a...?	donde se toma el autovús a ...?
How much is a ticket to ...?	¿Cuánto cuesta el pasaje a...?	kwanto kwesta el pasakhe a ...?
Is this the bus to ...?	¿Es éste el autobús a...?	es este el autovús a ...?
I am looking for this address.	Estoy buscando esta dirección...	estoy buskando esta direkthyón ...
At which station do I get off?	¿En qué estación tengo que bajar?	en ke estathyón tengo ke bakhar?

AIRPLANE / AVIÓN / ANYÓN

By which means of transport do I get to the airport?	¿Con qué medio de transporte puedo llegar al aeródromo?	kon ke medhio de transporte pwedho lyeghar al aeródromo?
Is there a bus service (taxi) to there?	¿Hay un servicio de autobús (taxi) hasta allí?	ai un servithio de autovús (taxi) asta alyi?
At what time will I be picked up?	¿A qué hora vendrán a buscarme?	a ke ora bendrán a buskarme?

English	Spanish	Pronunciation
Which is the nearest bus stop to the airport?	¿Cuál es la estación de autobús más cercana para el aeródromo?	kwal es la estathyón de autovús mas therkana para el aeródromo?
At what time should I be there?	¿A qué hora debo estar aquí?	a ke ora devo estar akí?
At what time does the plane take off?	¿A qué hora parte el avión?	a ke ora parte el avyón?
When will it arrive?	¿Cuándo llegará?	kwando lyeghará?
Is there a flight to?	¿Hay un vuelo a...?	ai un bwelo a ...?
What is the flight number?	¿Cuál es el número del vuelo?	kwal es el número de bwelo?
I have nothing to declare	No tengo nada para declarar	no tengo nadha para deklarar
This is all I have	Esto es todo lo que tengo	esto es todho lo ke tengo
Please, take my luggage	Por favor, lleve mi equipaje	por favor, lyeve mi ekipakhe
May I have a travel sickness pill, please?	¿Podría recibir una pastilla contra los mareos de viaje, por favor?	podhría rethivir una pastilya kontra los mareos de byakhe, por favor?
May I have a glass of water?	¿Podría recibir un vaso de agua?	podhría rethivir un baso de aghwa?

41

CAR JOURNEY	VIAJE EN AUTOMÓVIL	BYAKHE EN AUTOMÓVIL
Where can I rent a car?	¿Dónde puedo alquilar un automóvil?	donde pwedho alkilar un automóvil?
I have an international driving license	Tengo licencia de chofer internacional	tengo lithenthya de chofer internathyonal
How much is it to rent a car per day?	¿Cuánto cuesta alquilar un automóvil por día?	kwanto kwesta alkilar un automóvil por día?
What is the additional rate per kilometer?	¿Cuánto se debe agregar por kilómetro?	kwanto se deve aghreghar por kilómetro?
Where is the nearest petrol (gas) station?	¿Dónde está la estación de servicio más cercana?	donde está la estathyón de serbithyo mas therkana?
Please, put in ... liters	Sírvase echar...litros	sírbase echar ...litros
Check the oil, please	Sírvase revisar el aceite	sirbase revisar el atheite
... the brakes	... los frenos	...los frenos
... the gear box	... el embrague	...el embraghwe
Please put water in the battery; radiator	Sírvase echar agua en la batería, en el radiador	sirbase echar aghwa en la batería, en el radhyadhor

Change the oil in the car, please	Sírvase cambiar el engrase del automóvil	sírbase kambyar el engrase de automóvil
May I have a road map of the area?	¿Puedo recibir un mapa de los caminos de la región?	pwedho rethivir un mapa de los kaminos de la reghyón?
Please inflate the tires, the reserve wheel, too	Sírvase inflar las gomas, también la de la rueda de reserva	sírbase inflar las gomas, tambyén la de la rwedha de reserba
Please change the inner tube, the tire	Sírvase arreglar la pinchadura	sírbase arreglar la pinchadhura
Please repair the puncture	Por favor, cambie la cámara de la llanta	por favor, kambye la kámara de la lyanta
What is the speed limit?	¿Cuál es el máximo de velocidad permitida?	kwal es el máximo de belothidhadh permitidha?
Which is the way to ...	¿Cuál es el camino a...?	kwal es el kamino ...?
Is that a good road?	¿Es un camino bueno?	es un kamino bweno?
Is there a shorter way?	¿Hay un camino más corto?	ai un kamino mas korto?
Which place is this?	¿Qué lugar es éste?	ke lughar es éste?
Is this the road to ...?	¿Es éste el camino a...?	es éste el kamino a ...?
Yes, no	Sí, no	si, no

43

English	Spanish	Pronunciation
Please, go back	Por favor, retroceda	por favor, retrothedha
Go straight on	Siga derecho	sigha derecho
Turn to the right (left)	Diríjase a la derecha (a la izquierda)	dirikhase a la derecha (a la ithkyerda)
Turn to the north (south, east, west)	Diríjase al norte (sur, este, oeste)	dirikhase al norte (sur, este, oeste)
This way	Este camino	este kamino
That way	Aquel camino	akel kamino
How far is it to …?	¿A qué distancia está de…?	a ke distanthya está de …?
Is it near? (far?)	¿Está cerca? (¿lejos?)	está therka? (lekhos?)
Very far?	¿Muy lejos?	muy lekhos?
There, here	Allá, aquí	alyá, aki
Please, show me on the map	Por favor, muéstreme en el mapa	por favor, mwéstreme en el mapa
Where are we?	¿Dónde estamos?	donde estamos?
Where is the place that we want to go to?	¿Dónde está el lugar al que queremos llegar?	donde está el lughar al ke keremos lyeghar?
On which road should we travel?	¿Por qué camino debemos viajar?	por ke kamino devemos byakhar?

44

TRAFFIC SIGNS	SEÑALES DE TRÁFICO	SENYALES DE TRÁFIKO
Stop!	¡Pare!	pare!
Caution!	Cuidado	kwidhadho
Dangerous curve	Curva peligrosa	kurba peligrosa
Slow!	¡Despacio!	despathyo!
Danger!	¡Peligro!	peligro!
First Aid	Primeros auxilios	primeros auxilyos
Red Cross	Cruz Roja	kruth rokha
Pharmacy	Farmacia	farmathia
Police	Policía	polithia
Bomb disposal pit	Pozo para explosivos	potho para explosivos
Fire hydrant	Toma de agua para incendios	toma de aghwa para inthendyos
No parking	No hay estacionamiento	no ai estathyonamyento
No entry	Prohibida la entrada	proividha la entradha
No crossing	No cruzar	no kruthar
One-way Street	Calle de una sola mano	kalye de una sola mano

Pedestrian crossing	Paso para transeúntes	paso para transeúntes
Detour	Vuelta	bwelta
Men at work	Hombres trabajando	ombres travakhando
Right	Derecha	derecha
Left	Izquierda	ithkyerda
Entrance	Entrada	entradha
Exit	Salida	salidhà
No Smoking	¿Prohibido fumar!	prohividho fumar!
Information	Informaciones	informathyones
Elevator	Ascensor	asensor
Restrooms	Salas de descanso	salas de deskanso
Men	Hombres	ombres
Woman	Mujeres	mukheres
For sale	En venta	en benta
For rent	En alquiler	el alkiler
Travel on this road	¡Viaje por este camino!	byakhe por este kamino!
Travel slowly	¡Viaje despacio!	byakhe despathyo!
Take care	¡Tenga cuidado!	tenga kwidhadho!

English	Español	Pronunciation
Crossroad, junction, bridge	Cruce de caminos, bifurcación, puente	kruthe de kaminos, bifurkathyón, pwente
Highway, dual highway	Carretera, carretera doble	karretera, karretera doble
Bad road	Camino en malas condiciones	kamino en malas kondithyones
Narrow road	Camino angosto	kamino angosto
Road under repair	Camino en reparación	kamino en reparathyón
Dirt road	Camino de tierra	kamino de tyerra
Steep incline	Descenso en declive	desenso en deklive
Steep decline	Descenso empinado	desenso empinadho
Sharp turn	Vuelta brusca	bwelta bruska
Blinding light	Luz encandiladora	luth enkandiladhora
Children on the road	Niños en el camino	ninyos en el kamino

GARAGE / TALLER MECÁNICO / TALYER MEKÁNIKO

English	Español	Pronunciation
Where is a garage nearby?	¿Dónde hay un taller mecánico por aquí cerca?	donde ai un talyer mekániko por aki therka?
Please, check and adjust the brakes	Por favor, revise y arregle los frenos	por favor, revise i arreghle los frenos

47

English	Spanish	Phonetic
Please, check the gearbox and adjust the clutch	Sírvase revisar la caja de velocidades y ajustar el embrague	sírbase revisar la kakha de belothidhadhes i akhustar el el embraghwe
The engine uses too much oil	El motor consume demasiado aceite	el motor konsume demasyadho atheite
The engine is overheating	El motor está recalentado	el motor está rekalentadho
The radiator needs refilling too often	El radiador necesita que lo rellenen demasiado a menudo	el radhyadhor nethesita ke lo relyenen demasyadho a menudho
Please, check the plugs	Sírvase revisar los cojinetes	sírbase revisar los kokhinetes
Please, check the points	Sírvase revisar los metales	sírbase revisar los metales
The car doesn't start well	El auto no arranca bien	el auto no arranka byen
Please, check the headlight alignment	Sírvase revisar la dirección de las luces	sírbase revisar la direkthyón de las luthes

REPAIRS / REPARACIONES / REPARATHYONES

English	Spanish	Phonetic
Wheel balance	Equilibrio de ruedas	ekilibrio de rwedhas
Oil change	Cambio de aceite	kamyo de atheite

Tighten screws	Apretar los tornillos	apretar los tornilyos
Fill the radiator	Llene el radiador	lyene el radhyadhor
Oil the engine	Aceite el motor	atheite el motor
Wheel alignment	Ajuste de las ruedas	akhuste de las rwedhas
Water for the battery	Agua para la batería	aghwa para la batería
The gear is stuck	El engranaje está inerte	el engranakhe está inerte
…Coughing	…tosiendo	…tosiendo
The oil is leaking	El aceite está goteando	el atheite está goteando
The part is burnt out	La parte está ardiendo	la parte está ardyendo
To take a wheel apart	Tomar una rueda aparte	tomar una rwedha aparte
Short circuit	Corto circuito	korto thirkwito
The steering wheel is loose	El volante está suelto	el bolante está swelto
The axle rod is broken	La vara del eje está rota	la bara del ekhe está rota
Puncture in the tire	Una pinchadura en la llanta	una pinchadhura en la lyanta
Everything is O.K.	Todo está en orden	todho está en orden

PARTS OF A CAR	PARTES DE UN AUTOMÓVIL	PARTES DE UN AUTOMÓVIL
Battery	Batería	batería
Brakes	Frenos	frenos
Carburetor	Carburador	karburadhor
Clutch	Embrague	embraghwe
Distilled water	Agua destilada	aghwa destiladha
Filter	Filtro	filtro
Gear	Engranaje	engranakhe
Ignition	Encendido	enthendidho
Lubrication	Lubricación	lubrikathyón
Pedal	Pedal	pedhal
Piston	Pistón	pistón
Radiator	Radiador	radhyadhor
Spark plugs	Bujía de encendido	bukhia de enthendhidho, resorte
Spring	Resorte	
Steering wheel	Volante	bolante
Wheel, wheels	Rueda, ruedas	rwedha, rwedhas

PHYSICIANS	**MÉDICOS**	**MÉDHIKOS**
Where does an English speaking doctor live?	¿Dónde hay un médico que hable inglés?	donde ai un médhiko ke able ingles?
I need first aid	Necesito primeros auxilios	nethesito primeros auxilios
I need an internal specialist	Necesito un especialista en enfermedades internas	nethesito un espethialista en enfermedhadhes internas
Can you recommend a good doctor?	¿Puede recomendarme un buen médico?	pwedhe rekomendarme un bwen medhiko?

TYPES OF DOCTORS	**TIPOS DE MÉDICOS**	**TIPOS DE MÉDHIKOS**
Ear, nose and throat specialist	Especialista en oído, nariz y garganta	espethialista en oídho, narith i garghanta
Orthopedist	Ortopédico	ortopédhiko
Surgeon	Cirujano	thirukhano
Pediatrician	Pediatra	pedhiatra
Gynecologist	Ginecólogo	khinekólogho
Dermatologist	Dermatólogo	dermatólogho

English	Español	Pronunciation
Eye specialist	Especialista en ojos	espethialista en okhos
Neurologist	Neurólogo	neurólogho
Internal specialist	Especialista en enfermedades internas	espethialista en enfermedhadhes internas
Dentist	Dentista	dentista

ILLNESSES   MALESTAR   MALESTAR

I have no appetite	No tengo apetito	no tengo apetito
Nausea	Náusea	náusea
Infection	Infección	infekthyón
Depression	Depresión	depresyón
Cold	Resfriado	resfriadho
Vomiting	Vómitos	bómitos
Pregnancy, pregnant	Embarazo, embarazada	embaratho, embarathadha
Contraction	Contracción	kontrakthyón
Heart patient	Enfermo del corazón	enfermo del korathón
Fever	Fiebre	fyebre

PARTS OF THE BODY	PARTES DEL CUERPO	PARTES DEL KWERPO
Ankle, appendix	Tobillos, apéndice	tovilyos, apéndithe
Arm, artery	Brazo, arteria	bratho, arteria
Back, bladder	Espalda, vesicula	aspalda, besikula
Blood, bone	Sangre, hueso	sangre, weso
Breast, chest	Pecho, tórax	pecho, tórax
Ear, elbow	Oreja, codo	orekha, kodho
Eye, eyes	Ojo, ojos	okho, okhos
Finger	Dedo	dedho
Foot, feet	Pie, pies	pye, pyes
Gland	Glándula	glándula
Hand, head	Mano, cabeza	mano, kabetha
Heart, heel	Corazón, talón	korathón, talón
Hip, intestine	Cadera, intestino	kadhera, intestino
Joints, kidney	**Articulaciones, riñón**	artikulathyones, rinyon
Knee, leg	**Rodilla, pierna**	rodhilya, pyerna
Ligament, liver	**Ligamento, hígado**	lighamento, ighadho
Lungs, mouth	Pulmones, boca	pulmones, boka

Muscle, neck	Músculo, cuello	múskulo, kwelyo
Nerve, nerves	Nervio, nervios	nerbyo, nerbyos
Nose	Nariz	narith
Palm	Palma	pálma
Rib, shoulder	Costilla, hombro	kostilya, ombro
Skin, spine	Piel, columna dorsal	pyel, kolumna dorsal
Stomach, throat	Estómago, garganta	estómagho, garghanta
Thumb, tongue	Pulgar, lengua	pulghar, lengwa
Tooth, teeth	Diente, dientes	dyente, dyentes
Tonsil	Amígdala	amigdala
Urine, vein	Orina, vena	orina, bena

PHARMACY	FARMACIA	FARMATHÍA
Where is the nearest pharmacy?	¿Dónde está la farmacia más cercana?	donde está la farmathía mas therkana?
Which pharmacy is on duty tonight?	¿Cuál farmacia está de turno esta noche?	kwal farmathía está de turno esta noche?
Have you a medicine for a headache?	¿Tiene un remedio para el dolor de cabeza?	tyene un remedhio para el dolor de kabetha?
Toothache	Dolor de muelas	dolor de mwelas
Iodine; Aspirin	Yodo, aspirina	yodho, aspirina
Valerian drops	Gotas valerianas	gotas baleryanas
Antiseptic cream	Crema antiséptica	krema antiséptika
Hot water bottle	Una botella de agua	una botelya de aghwa
Heating pad	Almohadóm eléctrico	almo'adhón eléktriko
Cottonwool, band-aid	Algodón absorbente, cinta plástica	alghodhón absorbente, thinta plástika
Thermometer	Termómetro	termómetro
I need first aid	Necesito primeros auxilios	nethesito primeros auxilyos
What are his office hours?	¿Cuáles son las horas de la oficina?	kwales son las oras de la ofithina?

TIME	**TIEMPO**	**TYEMPO**
What is the time? It is four o'clock	¿Qué hora es? Son las cuatro	ke ora es? son las kwarto
Five minutes past six, half past five	Las seis y cinco, las cinco y media	las ses i thinko, las thinko i medhya
A quarter past seven, ten minutes to eight	Las siete y cuarto, las ocho menos diez	las syete i kwarto, las ocho menos dyeth
Morning	Mañana	manyana
Midday, afternoon	Mediodía, tarde	medhyodhía, tarde
Evening, night	Anochecer, noche	anochether, noche,
Midnight	Medianoche	medhyanoche
Today	Hoy	oy
Yesterday	Ayer	ayer
The day before yesterday	Antes de ayer	antes de ayer
Tomorrow	Mañana	manyana
The day after tomorrow	Pasado mañana	pasedho manyana
A second, hour	Un segundo, hora	un seghundo, ora
Quarter of an hour	Cuarto de hora	kwarto de ora

English	Español	Pronunciation
Half and hour	Media hora	medhya ora
Forty minutes	Cuarenta minutos	kwarenta minutos
Day, days	Día, días	dia, dias
Week, weeks	Semana, semanas	semana, semanas
Month, months	Mes, meses	mes, meses,
Year, years	Año, años	anyo, anyos
Period of... years	Periodo de... años	periodho de... anyos
In a month	En un mes	en un mes
Early, I am early	Temprano, me anticipé	temprano, me antithipé
Late, I am late	Tarde, me atrasé	tarde, me atrasé

DAYS OF THE WEEK

LOS DÍAS DE LA SEMANA

LOS DÍAS DE LA SEMANA

Sunday, Monday	Domingo, lunes	domingo, lunes
Tuesday, Wednesday	Martes, miércoles	martes, myérkoles
Thursday, Friday	Jueves, viernes	khweves, byernes
Saturday	Sábado	sávadho

57

MONTHS	**MESES**	**MESES**
January, February	Enero, febrero	enero, febrero
March, April	Marzo, abril	martho, abril
May, June	Mayo, junio	mayo, khunyo
July, August	Julio, agosto	khulyo, aghosto
September, October	Septiembre, octubre	septyembre, oktubre
November, December	Noviembre, diciembre	novyembre, dithyembre

SEASONS	**ESTACIONES**	**ESTATHYÓNES**
Spring, summer	Primavera, verano	primavera, berano
Autumn, winter	Otoño, invierno	otonyo, inbyerno

NUMBERS	**NÚMEROS**	**NÚMEROS**
One, two	Uno, dos	uno, dos
Three, four	Tres, cuatro	tres, kwatro
Five, six	Cinco, seis	thinko, ses

58

Seven, eight	Siete, ocho	syete, ocho
Nine, ten	Nueve, diez	nweve, dyeth
Eleven, twelve	Once, doce	onthe, dothe
Thirteen, fourteen	Trece, catorce	trethe, katorthe
Fifteen, sixteen	Quince, dieciséis	kinthe, dyethises
Seventeen, eighteen	Diecisiete, dieciocho	dyethisyete, dyethiocho
Nineteen, twenty	Diecinueve, veinte	dyethinweve, beynte
Twenty one, twenty two	Veinitiuno, veintidós	bentiuno, bentidhos
Thirty, forty	Treinta, cuarenta	treynta, kwarenta
Fifty, sixty, seventy	Cincuenta, sesenta, setenta	thinkwenta, sesenta, setenta
Eighty, ninety, one hundred	Ochenta, noventa, cien	ochenta, noventa, thyen
One hundred and one	Ciento uno	thyento-uno
Two hundred	Doscientos	dosthyentos
One thousand	Mil	mil
One thousand and on	Mil uno	mil uno
Two thousand	Dos mil	dos mil
Two thousand and one	Dos mil uno	dos mil uno
One million	Un millón	un milyón
One billion	Mil millones	mil milyones

EMERGENCY EXPRESSIONS	LLAMADOS DE URGENCIA	LYAMADHOS DE URKHENTHÍA
Help!	¡Socorro!	sokorro!
Thief!	¡Ladrones!	ladhrones!
Stop, thief!	¡Deténgase, ladrón!	deténgase, ladrón!
Don't touch me!	¡No me toque!	no me toke!
Leave me alone!	¡Déjeme solo!	dékheme solo!
Call the police!	¡Llame a la policia!	lyame a la polithía!
I've lost my way.	Me encuentro perdido	me enkwentro perdidho
Call me a taxi, please	Llámeme un taxi, por favor	lyámeme un taxi, por favor
Take me to this address.	Lléveme a esta dirección	lyéveme a esta direkthyón
I don't feel well.	No me siento bien	no me syento byen
Call a doctor!	¡Llame a un médico!	lyame a un médhiko!
Call an ambulance!	¡Llame una ambulancia!	lyame una ambulanthia!
Take me to a first-aid station.	¡Lléveme a una estación de primeros auxilios!	lyéveme a una estathyón de primeros auxilyos!
Take me to the hospital.	Lléveme al hospital	lyéveme al ospital
Take me to a doctor.	Lléveme a un médico	lyéveme a un médhiko